EGG/SHELL

Victoria Kennefick grew up in Cork and lives in Kerry. Her debut collection, *Eat or We Both Starve* (Carcanet Press, 2021), won the Seamus Heaney First Collection Poetry Prize and the Dalkey Book Festival Emerging Writer of the Year Award. It was shortlisted for the T.S. Eliot Prize, the Costa Poetry Book Award, Derek Walcott Prize for Poetry, and the Butler Literary Prize. She was the UCD/Arts Council of Ireland Writer in Residence 2023 and Poet-in-Residence at the Yeats Society Sligo 2022-2024. Her poems have appeared in *Poetry Magazine*, *New England Review*, *PN Review*, *The Poetry Review*, *Poetry London*, *Poetry Ireland Review*, *The Stinging Fly*, and elsewhere.

egg /
shell

victoria kennefick

CARCANET POETRY

First published in Great Britain in 2024 by
Carcanet
Alliance House, 30 Cross Street
Manchester, M 2 7 A Q
www.carcanet.co.uk

Paperback I S B N 978 1 80017 383 5
Hardback I S B N 978 1 80017 387 3 (Limited Edition)

Book design by Andrew Latimer, Carcanet
Typesetting by LiteBook Prepress Services
Printed in Great Britain by SRP Ltd, Exeter, Devon

The publisher acknowledges financial
assistance from Arts Council England.

CONTENTS

/SHELL

For V

'I fell in love with a swan.
My eyes were filled with feathers.'

– from 'Lord of the Reedy River' (Donovan, arr. Kate Bush)

'…who would believe that they could come from the inside of an
egg, if he did not know that it happened?'

– Ovid, *Metamorphoses*, trans. by Mary M. Innes (1955)

EGG/SHELL

RAM

It's on the kitchen table,
the ram's skull.

He came in cradling it in his arms, *Don't worry,*
it's been dead for ages, he whispered, then touched my cheek,
a circuit forming between him, me, and the Ram
that flooded my body with crackling winter fire.

He plonked the skull down
before vanishing,

as he does, into his head and left this head,
still on the wood, just bone and horns.
And oh, what horns! I imagine his admirers' eyes –
dark slits expanding to take them all in.

The curve of them,
looping, intentional things –

ridged, strong – I can't look for long, can't reach out
to touch them though it's all I want to do.
To be honest, I am scared – of the narrow brittle skull
between two magnificent coronets –

a sliver of bone, and in its empty
sockets, a black blankness.

It is the devil, no doubt, here on our kitchen table
like a vase. It vibrates, I can almost hear its ancient bleats.
Every time I make tea, load the dishwasher, stack plates,
it is there –

weird
exhibit –

I'll take it to show her, he says when he returns,
meaning our two-year-old who has been asking about bones,
can smell death in the house. She runs in,
her teething cheeks hot and red,

Mama, the baa baa doesn't need
its head anymore.

The three of us and the Ram –
its presence a whisper from the future,
stubborn, yes, and unapologetic. It's on the table even now.
Tomorrow it will disappear to his laboratory

but tonight, I can't stop thinking about
those hollow orbs –

the thin fragments of skull clinging
together to give shape to an idea –
Ram, silhouetted against all the objects, against
all the light. Ram, who am I supposed to be in all this –

the floral blinds, the recipe books, the porcelain floor tiles?
Oh Ram, let us bash our heads off them and weep.

EGG/

CHICKEN

At night I dream of chickens.
In this first year of marriage, I am deranged.

In the dreams, I try to teach the poultry to touch type
while they insist on giving birth at my feet.

They're impossible so I swallow
their eggs whole. They hatch inside

until I ovum my mouth, downy full-stops pop out –
a magic trick I do at the end of sentences.

Should I chop off their heads with an axe? Maybe.
Arrange the corpses to look like they're flying? Perhaps.

Or I carry their skulls in my pockets like clanking marbles, stuff
yellow fluff up my nose, breathe feathers.

Oh, but they enact their revenge before the alarm goes off,
peck me into a board like a key until I spell something out.

Or shrink me until I am no bigger than a seed. Or I dream
that I survive for weeks after my head's cut off.

I scream, *CHICKEN!*
I want to count every last one of the paltry lot.

Tell me about it, my husband says, plucking feathers
from my hair like air quotes, or sleep.

I want to tell him, I do. But I'm all out of luck
so I cluck, and cluck, and cluck –

Gallus gallus domesticus.

NIGHTBABY

I've never thought about the moon so much,
considered it sister-like, watching us learn
how to be together. You in my arms, perfect
circle of your small mouth pressed to my breast.
Lunar light from my phone, my own brain, the moon
all shining. It's scary how big the night is, how small
we are in it. Think of the others up with us,
a night-nation of milk and mouths all fumbling
towards each other in the dark, singing.
The shape of you, a crescent against me. Little planet
exploring your phases. Oh, moon be good to her
in the ebb-and-flow of monthly life. Lick the path clean.
But for now sweet Nightbaby, rock with me.

LULLABY!

She lay down like a lamb,
in the end. In my fists
my hair, pulled out in clumps.
I listen to her breath.
steady in the cot, sweet as milk.
Lock-jawed, light-headed,
I want to drift. All is quiet,
all is quiet, you hear?

But cars growl like monsters
under the window
(what are you trying to do to me?)

The tuneless hiss of radios slithers
under door cracks, through
a careless open window.

Dogs bound around the green, yap
in packs. I want to slice off their long,
dangling tongues. (Where is my knife?)

Wind, enough! Cease tapping the blackout blind,
gossiping about me in Morse code.
(I am a good mother.)

Birds, not you too. Each peep
stabs my palms. Don't you have babies
awake at 5am, cheeping at such a pitch
the very sky shakes itself awake,
blinking. It's bloody eye open,
ready or not? SHUT UP. I bite
down on a towel. My baby,
(my baby), she's wide awake now.

ON BEING TWO IN THE ANTHROPOCENE

I am a sea and you are a bird.
You're not a baby but a big girl holding my face
in your soft little claws. You are lark and you are singing, *Hello!*
Mama and baba – or big girl – rocking like we used to.
     You are a bird, a baby, a baby bird all cosy,
     only to leap off my rock-nest and blow kisses
     to house spiders. *I am not scared of them,* you say.
I am not scared of them, I parrot. (I think that's what
you're supposed to do. Echo them.) *We like spiders,* I say.
They live with us. I have shown you their webs
hugging corners of cloudy windows. Beyond
     our little thumbprint of garden lies unmowed.
     It is the bugs' house, we must not squash them, you say.
     And butterflies! Why do they wear make-up, mama?
I am conscious then of my face, of what I hide
with my face. All summer your chubby cheeks are slicked white
with sunscreen. There's your hat tossed like a petal on the grass.
The neighbours pass, we explain our untended plot
     is intentional. They smile and nod.
     We tell the caretaker to skip our patch. I still run
     after you, pick things up. When you nap, I watch
the snip, snip, snip. When you don't, we walk slow loops
around the wetlands. *I get sad when they cut the grass,* you pipe up,
your hand glued to mine. *I do too,* I say. *That is a magpie,*
one for sorrow. Always wave it away. You are tired, I carry you.
     I imitate lark sounds. It is not enough.
     The nests are empty.
     I get sad when hedgerows are ripped out
like insulation from a rotting house.
I get sad as earth becomes sea. I get sad
that in showing you this sinking world
I teach you how to say goodbye.

I chase you around the house at your request, holding up the dragon mask you made at playschool in front of my face. You shine a torch in my eyes, scream because you want to. Run into the arm of your father because you can. Lately, we have been inundated with questions about ogres and dinosaurs, trolls, and great white sharks. All of them monsters and as real or imaginary as you wish them to be. Wolves aren't real for example, they're only in stories with their sharp, glistening teeth ready to gouge Red's delicate head – so don't worry. But at night you toss and turn, wake up and shout out in the dark, unnamed shadows stalk you. It's easy to soothe you. I never knew my larynx held such cooing sounds, little inflections, and soon you snooze again. I go back to bed, your father's warm body, his arms flung over to my side, oblivious. I lie awake thinking about monsters, big and small, especially ones that don't look like monsters at all. How we'll keep them away, hold them back. The darkness is thick as melted wax. Let's find the wick, I'll light it and you hold it up, quick.

TEACHING MY DAUGHTER HOW TO BREAK AN EGG

She hesitates. She who is told not to break, who is asked
did she break or why did she break.

    Go for it, I tell her. She looks at me and taps,
Harder, I say. She laughs and raps. It shatters,
not a clean break but tiny catastrophic fissures, miniature tiles,

    a mosaic of destruction. Once more, and the insides spill out.
The yolk is punctured and brilliant orange.
We smile at each other; her fingers are sticky. She hates that.

    I do too. We wash our hands together under the cold tap,
wipe them dry on a tea towel. Now, we make sure to stir the egg
into the mixture so all the ingredients are indistinguishable.

    We plop it in the tin, the gloopy mess, push it
into the oven's hot womb. There it will solidify into an edible brick
for us to break again. But now all can I say is,

    Careful, careful you don't get burned.

THE WILD SWANS AT THE WETLANDS CENTRE

Just one swan: her perfect twin floating
beneath, a trick. She dips her beak into herself, hoping not
to meet water but the soft plumage of another.

The incident described in detail by the Centre staff –
how her partner fell from the sky, crashed into the path.
A mess – brains, blood, feathers, screams. A quick clean-up.

I wish I had been there,
it is so colourless somedays.

Bereft and haunted, she lollops up
the rocks to her island nest, gathers her neck into a sleeping *S*.
We visit often, there is nothing else to do

until one day there are two. Her new partner has a strong,
plump body, an insistent beak. He is very protective.
We watch them for weeks.

You scoot around the lake ahead of me,
delighted by your new-found autonomy.

Come spring, and your birthday, they assemble
an untidy heap of reeds and grass
close to the water's edge, a present.

The cob sits on the nest guarding the precious orbs
while she feeds in cold water by the pedal boats, then incubates.
She almost never leaves them.

This morning there was blood in the toilet water,
I cannot seem to keep them.

The cob hisses at toddlers and a knobbly-kneed man.
We worry, what if there is a flood, or mink attack, or that pointy
heron standing sentry-like on the bridge gets hungry.

I am afraid of what has happened, the swans' necks droop low.
We watch our own water-selves tag along, until one day
she's left the nest. No downy fluff, no little brood. Nothing.

I have nothing to show, kneeling at the lip of the lake
alone in the evening, wringing my hands.

I touch its cold body. They approach,
we split on liquid, become part of each other
while broken slithers of streetlight and moon, unreachable

in monochrome, repeat themselves
over and over us and onto the water.

NO. ONE: IVY

I once wore a wreath of ivy to ward off intoxication
from alcohol and other dangers.

I once wore a wreath of ivy
to be closer to poetry, as if it were a place.

So, when you came into being, little sprout, so loyal
and eager, I could feel you immediately

shoring me up from the inside. I was carrying the world –
so fragile, this future predated by a timeline of cramps.

Ivy in my wedding bouquet gesturing to fidelity
which would turn out to be the least of my worries.

Ivy looped and luscious around trees that formed
a guard of honour on the bus to Dublin

on a school trip to the theatre. How glamorous.
I stood in the gap between seats making announcements

when there was a little shift, a little – alteration.
I couldn't rearrange my face, but kept a teacher's grin,

breezy, breezy – *Come on everyone, line up in twos.*
That's what we do. Later in the auditorium

lights down low, I scooched past students in the row
propped on red velvet seats, then struggled through

huge doors to the plush bathrooms, mirrored, mirroring
spots of scarlet on my gusset, blood on the tissue.

It was January, bleak and hollow. I was
January suffocated by ivy. It took two days. I even

went to school. That's what we do. At the end, I put
your big sister to bed, kissed her curls, took myself

to give birth in a grave; tears fell into the toilet too.
Then I laughed at how pathetic I was, and so alone.

Winter Ivy down the bowl, here I am smashed on
cold tiles, a broken cup, useless to you.

Winter Ivy, here I am drunk and stupid, trying to live
in a poem, trying to hold words like pills.

Winter Ivy, you are choking me, who cannot hold anything,
not even your father's hand.

ODE TO SELF-LOATHING

O little knife
O tiny knife
pin more like
how do i carry you in this life?
why do i break my own heart
over & over & over
pin cushion with legs
angry cookie
bad voodoo doll impersonator

snip snip,
i am in pieces
imagining other brains
appraising me
but it's my brain
you see
who cares what you think of me?
what do i think of me?
    – O Pain! –
    – O unbearable sadness –
you are such a prick

ARE YOU GOING TO HAVE ANOTHER BABY?

I am that woman you're afraid of.
　　　My reptilian eyes dart to the plump face
of your freshly born baby.
　　　Yes, I want it! My toddler skitters at my feet,
recognises the signs – the slowing
　　　of my heartbeat, the flick
of my long, thin tongue.
　　　I don't want to pine, I want to die
of longing for the doughy body
　　　of a toothless child clung to me,
dribbling absolution down
its double chins. Oh, let me.
Let me take it – I'll tend it well –
　　　See, see (Show off dear! Prance
　　　　　　　　　　　for the lady and the baby!)
　　　Marvel at how efficiently,
how quickly I made *this* child
　　　(All the other ones died, all
　　　　　　　　　the other ones died.)
I deserve another still warm
　　　crawling towards me
on the mat – what do you
　　　think of that? You'll hardly miss
this one, they say you'll still be a mother –
　　　and as old as you are,
I'm sure you'll have another –

AND ANOTHER THING

they do not tell you   about what happens   to your body

when it makes one more   is that your gums get redder   grow so angry

they turn against your teeth   (blithely tucked up in their plushy bed)   and push them   out

                        inflamed and raging

is a nursing mother safer   when she's toothless?

I DO AN EGG CLEANSE BECAUSE I MUST

You might do an egg cleanse if you are feeling a bit off.
I feel unlucky and sad. I do an egg cleanse.
In a bowl I clean the egg of any negative energy,
add a spoonful of salt, then a squeeze of lemon juice.

I wash it gently; I say a prayer.
Please help me, please help me, please.
I rinse the egg and dry it with a towel,
it's as bald as a baby so I cradle it.

Next, I fill a glass quarter way up
then hold the egg in my hands.
It warms and I blow my intention
onto it, all the things I'd like to get rid of.

With this cleanse I free myself of bad energy!
With this cleanse I will no longer have rotten luck!
With this cleanse I will make the right decisions!
With this cleanse my life will return to me as it was!

It's time to sit down then. Holding the egg in one hand
I rub it along the back of my head, then to my ears,
and my hot, tired face. I close my eyes and smooth it
along the lids, across my lonely lips too.

I go from head to toe –
the egg is taking it all away, the bad energy,
the mistakes, the delusions, the incessant weeping,
the feelings of helplessness, the rage –

time to crack. Into the glass goes the yolk.
I wait for things to settle,
peer through to see the shape of it.
The colour oozes to fill the container.

Smelly water or blood: there may be evil spirits around me!
Bubbles: negative energy was absorbed into the egg!
Cobwebs in the whites: I may have an evil eye on me!
A face in the yolk: I have an enemy!

It doesn't matter what I see, or which way I look,
because even though I beg for grace and
frantically search out for space,
there is still so much egg on my stupid face.

NO. TWO: FERN

We went to the zoo.
It was what they call
a close day so your big
sister's treacle-coloured
curls were stuck to
her forehead like
question marks.
My hands were swollen,
you were only a tiny
frond inside me – but I
felt heavy watching lions
flick their tails
behind glass.
How powerless
they seemed, or rather
how dormant the
dominance, how they
could unleash
their wildness without
warning. The thrill of that
knowledge, the fear of it,

made me breathless.
We went to the
playground,
your sister scrambled up
climbing frames
and squeaked down
slides, her little thighs
sticking to the metal
slowed her down.
Later, in the café to order
lunch, I couldn't make
sense of the food
displayed. Slabs, grated
pieces, slices. The words
on the blackboard,
all those curlicues and
flourishes slid off the
slate into a heap.
*Are you okay? What can I
get you?* a swingy
ponytail asked.

The queue lengthened,
I didn't know what to
choose, what to eat,
what to feed my baby.
I ran back to the table,
someone ordered us
sandwiches, I ate mine
like a chastened child,
each bite dry.
Tears jammed,
formed a fist in my throat.
I don't remember any-
thing, but in the morning
every tear turned
red, nightmares liquified
and you escaped,
wild child, back
to your element.
I watched my future
disappear again
contained behind glass.

MOUSIE

To name a garment – a nasty
polyester nightie at that –
Mousie
was a strange move
but it felt like someone to me.
My eight-year-old self a walking mannequin
to Mousie's antics, begging
for cheese from her mother – while behind
the toadstool, the blades
of grass and the fall
of the fabric –
my body was telling a story of its own,
growing out and up
at such an alarming rate
that by summertime
Mousie didn't fit over my breasts.
I cried. How could my own
body betray me,
rebel like some rat.
My mother sewed in little darts
and panels to ease the change.
Now my tiny daughter wears it, and asks
what these are for, and these,
to the patches and stitches
and I tell her
just you wait.

NO. THREE: WILLOW

Alone, my pale belly
is exposed and all jelly.
Stuck on my back,
I'm loose as a sack,
I see you wiggle
on the ultrasound,
imagine you being
so large, potbound.
You, a mere twig,
newly stuck in the ground—
who knows what
miracles can abound.
See, your tiny heart beating!
I can almost imagine us meeting,
my baby, my baby, Willow,
it's you. I thought I was one,
but now I am two.
I turn to the sonographer,
smiling. I want to shout, it's all fine –
see that baby, it's mine!

What an idiot.
She shakes her head, tuts even.
The sac is small. Come back
in three days. I don't
bother, it's all over in two.

O BRIGID, O EXALTED ONE, LISTEN TO MY PLEA
AS I CELEBRATE YOU

(whispers)

Remember
she is only the size of a strawberry seed,
of a bristle on a toothbrush.
Tiny, tadpole-like
with a tail
growing –

Flame-haired, you are in the damp grass, Brigid.
Your pale hands cradle me, cup me like water.
I lick across your palms, molecules of me expecting
to reassemble a newborn body, fluid and fresh.
Goddess of wells, Goddess of wombs
and words and the first light of morning,
carry me to where I can spring forth.
      Pour me into the stream so I flow,
      use me to cool the red-hot
      iron of your smithing – all sunlight and fire.
      Help me to rise like you though I fall,
      to surge through it all –
      gush over dry stone. Heal me,
      let me keep this seed safe, deliver it
wrapped in your cloak, fully-grown to the earth.
I don't want to keen anymore, my throat
dry from the emptiness in my arms.
I don't want to give this one back. I drop
coins in the river, leave an apple at its lip
and on the bank the bread that failed to rise.
I will cross and recross myself with grass and sticks –
      three-armed and ready for battle with whatever

wants to take my babies from me.
Now you're wading in with me and mine, Brigid.
The red line of dawn slaps blue water,
a confluence, and you will hold us all
in flame and wave,
won't you?

CUP

I restore it in my head though my head is one, it overflowed in the deep sink
in the tiny kitchen overlooking the rose garden. There, painted presses slid along
little grooves to reveal what remained of my grandmother's fine bone china
tea set. A few saucers, a squat jug with fluted spout, this cup that was my
favourite. The porcelain so thin I could see the shadow of my finger
through it, the intricate spindle of the handle kissed with gold ferns,
hand-painted with posies, cerise, with petals like tiny fans or
feathers. How I worried for it, whose lip wanted other lips.
I hold it now, in two hands like a careful child; it's so
light, lighter than an egg, light as light and sunlight
diffuses through its membrane filling its bowl
like a baby bird's beak, wide then narrow.
On the draining board it barely makes
a sound; the dust curls up inside and
at the bottom, I only see it now,
the crack, barely there but
enough to make this
useless as a cup.
It doesn't know what it is now, a vessel for missing buttons, knotted chains, random
batteries. No more tealeaves telling the future. The crack doesn't widen, the cup doesn't
break. Is it, or isn't it, still a cup? Its lifeline getting longer, its fault-line looking up.

POTION

Naturally inclined to witchcraft in the way of most children,
alone in the garden my daughter makes a potion from:
rainwater,
flowerheads and sticks,
an empty snail shell (deep as an ear canal),
     small rocks,
and grass.
The more elaborate concoctions
require
pulled-up roots,
     weary petals ground on the path to turn the water pink,
strands of my salt-and-pepper hair pulled out with tiny, furious fists.
     (At least she prays to trees for their permission to use bark.)
After storms
she hunts for fallen eggs
to add to the mixture,
     the lump in my throat ovum-shaped,
ready to crack.
     She only harvests rotten ones,
they have more magic, she maintains,
     I think only of the embryo decaying.
Sometimes, she catches
     the frantic sounds of the parent birds
in her skirt—
     but they are too sad to use most days.
Potions and soup she likes to serve
in her play pool,
     a bucket,
flowerpots,
     a dog bowl,

in a deep hole she dug in the garden.
       Bundles of long grasses, leaves,
other treasures she ties to low hanging branches
       or places in the nook of a rock.
She aggressively offers mud and dandelions
       to any worm she sees. Today she's perfected a love potion,
yesterday a poison for enemies.
       The antidote is to eat bugs or store rocks in the mouth.
She is very knowledgeable. I tell her so
       as she fills her baby doll's bottle
with an elixir to make a baby sister.

INCOMPLETE RECIPE FOR CUSTARD

Prep:10 mins
Cook:15 mins

Easy

Serves 8

Once you've cracked this technique
for silky smooth vanilla custard
you'll never go back.

BAD EGG

Almost everyone has been faced with this conundrum —
you reach into the fridge for an egg, but can't
remember how long they have been squatting there.
Over time, an egg's quality declines as the air pocket inside
gets larger and the whites thinner. An egg only goes bad
when it starts to decompose due to bacteria

or mould. Your eggs may be good
to eat for many more weeks. When in doubt,
you can find out with a simple sniff.
Or, in addition to your nose,
your eyes can be used to check
that the shell is not cracked, slimy or powdery.
Much like ascertaining if a woman is a witch,

the float test is also a common method for determining
the age of a fertilised egg. Gently set your egg
into a bowl of water. If the egg sinks,
it is fresh. If it tilts upwards or even floats,
it is old. Ta-dah! Candling is a method
used either to assess the quality of a table egg or
the development of the chick
in a fertilised egg. Hold the light source up

to the large end of the egg. Tilt it and turn
quickly from left to right. The contents of the egg
should be illuminated. A lack of knowledge about how
to tell when an egg has gone bad leads some people
to needlessly throw away good eggs. Don't forget
that even if an egg passes these tests, it's important
to fully cook it to a safe temperature before you eat it.
And please know, despite all your efforts,

there will always be one.

NO. FOUR: SAGE

I took the drugs,
shared my news,
gave up coffee,
stayed away from the news.
You slipped away slowly.
Each day, a little more
until you were nowhere.
Why doesn't my body
forget? I am still eating
for two, my waistband cuts
into the flesh of my waist.
I mean, my waste.

WILD SWANS AGAIN

Pregnant again,
the swans are nesting again.
We're going around and around

the lake
at the wetlands again.
Waiting again.

But this time there are eight cygnets!
Your high, clear laughter
at the joy of it bursts through

the grey clouds hanging
around the mountain's shoulders.
Maybe this is a sign, I think.

There were only two adult swans
in the water, but I saw four.
Another omen, nice and even.

And seeing how the water doesn't
soak the feathers, the swans'
plumage is never wet.

Imagine going through the world
like that? Untouched, gliding,
so very, very bright.

They say in Hinduism that
a swan, offered a mixture of
milk and water, can drink the milk

in isolation. To be that discerning,
to be able to make a choice
and follow through.

In the distance, Blennerville Windmill
rotates its blades, sending empty
sharp kisses to the sky.

Observation

–   Chick death at any stage   *Oh God.*

<u>Possible Causes</u>

–   Infection: Either the incubator is contaminated   *(Corrupted –)*
    or the egg itself was contaminated outside.
    Darkening around the yolk sack and a foul
    smell –

<u>Solutions</u>

–   Disinfect the incubator   *I shower every day.*

Observation

–   Chicks hatch earlier than expected   *Still, they fall out.*

<u>Possible Causes</u>

–   Incubation temperature too high   *Hot cramps*

<u>Solutions</u>

–   Reduce the incubation temperature somewhat   *I cannot stop.*
    (0.5° C)

Observation

–   Chicks hatch later than expected   *I waited, I waited,*

Possible Causes

–   Incubation temperature too low   *shivering in bed socks,*

Solutions

–   Increase the incubation temperature somewhat   *for it to be over.*
    (0.5° C)

Observation

–   Hatching times far apart   *Seven weeks.*

Possible Causes

–   Different development phases based on differing   *Six weeks.*
    storage periods or fluctuations of the incubation   *Eight weeks (with*
    temperature   *heartbeat)*
       Seven weeks.

Solutions

–   Limit the time storage periods of the eggs   *Get tested.*
–   Ensure a steady incubation period – avoid direct   *Take folic acid.*
    sun.   *Progesterone.*

Observation

–   Generally poor results   *They keep dying.*

<u>Possible Causes</u>

- Incorrect incubation settings
- Poor health of the parents
- Insufficient turning of the eggs

I am all static
(Of course)
I spin around and

<u>Solutions</u>

- Correct the incubation settings
- Improve the health of the parents
- Analyse the weight loss of the eggs
- Turn eggs more frequently

I am trying,
I am trying.
Tupperware coffin.
We try again.

FAILED TRANSLATION OF A PIGEON'S COO

I have been eavesdropping on the pigeons,
literally. They gather in pairs on the windowsill,
under the eaves, their wing beats like whirring screams,
making noises that no pigeons of my previous acquaintance
have ever made before. They don't know I am here.
Lately I've had the feeling that nature's been trying
to talk to me and maybe choosing pigeons to do so.
How to discern the needs of birds – there is nothing
wrong with them as far as I can tell. The feeders
attracted them, the sunflower seeds scattered to the ground
in the wind like careless punctuation, mostly tiny commas.
I listen to the cacophony of screeches and whines.
They can't be hungry. They seem more like acquaintances
than lovers, though when did that ever stop a bird.
Is it important, what they're saying? I'm dying
to tell them I already know what's coming down
on us – a creeping silence of sky.

A CHILD'S FIRST EXPERIENCE OF PLANTING SEEDS

> *...eggs fall from the shelves*
> *eggs walk away*
> 'Egg' by Wong May

The children grow cress from eggs,
          the inside scooped out and clean
enough for the cotton ball to pop in.
          A poor replacement.

Then they drop seeds on top, tiny as lice,
          and a little water. How come
it is so easy for these fragile stems to
grow and leaf, barely rooted
in a cloud contained within

a broken, useless thing?
They draw smiley faces on
the shell, learning
how seemingly simple it is to

make things grow.

LE CYGNE, MY SPIRIT ANIMAL

What do you call it? An affinity?
That I have sought out swans,
that they have sought me out.
Gloria – my pet
swan among a dozen others –
I remember flinging
my child-self out the sunroof
of my father's car hurtling
down the road to the beach
to see you. I swore I could identify you-
graceful, keener, lamentably
more awkward on land.

Years later, I went to a fortune-teller
in Galway, a favour to a friend
who never showed up. Left
to hear my fate alone, she said –
You will be disappointed. I am
disappointed. *You will meet a swan.*
Your spirit animal is a swan.
Easy to say when I told her
about Gloria. I tell everyone
everything. It's a compulsion.
I want people
to know me, and to hide.

The fortune teller told me
to focus on a swan's legs
underneath the water,
on the elegance of the swan
never letting on the effort it takes

to look so serene. My friend said,
She saw you coming!
But the next day, when I emerged
from the cathedral's mouth
there was my swan, distraught,
lolloping towards the traffic.
And you, holding my hand,

knew what to do and with your coat
shooed the swan back to the car park.
We called Swan Rescue, their posters
feathering the lampposts. You held her
in the blanket they threw to you
while the swan became very still.
A hook in her mouth, poor thing.
I was terrified, scared of animals then,
their muteness, tense until
she was sedated by the volunteer
who thanked us for our service,
took her away bundled in the back
of a small transit van.

We rescued her. You rescued her,
but she couldn't rescue us
and you listened to the tape
of the fortune teller lying
next to me as the boundaries between
us dissolved like sugar in water
until we couldn't tell each other apart.
I was cut, you were bleeding.

It's so long ago it doesn't matter,
except I am sorry for showing you
how fast my legs paddled through

the heavy river, there was no need
for you to see that, or for you to
display your own clock's workings
But *hiss*, *hiss*, what about swans
that spit, attack, wings outstretched.
This reticence doesn't work either.
And on I swim, and on, Gloria.
Neck high, feather's dry.

HALLOWEEN

Please don't egg my house, can't you see I'm already walking
on eggshells?

PAPER *THIN*

Torn leaf pressed flat
on earth's chest,

a palm
resuscitating its quiet pulse,

this sprawl
that creeps in spring,

a thirst so that April rains,
though icy and unknowable,

fickle as any scan of sky,
must fall. Trees' linen

barks crease as our own skins
fold into unfamiliar versions

of ourselves re-
writing outlines as summer sucks

on hay bales. We try,
on the beach, to read

braille of bird claw,
of our own footprints, if we look

behind us, if we double-check.
We search these woods,

the shore,
tilled fields, pavement – hinterlands

of yearning,
endlessly. Why do we crumple

like paper
with the wrong words written down?

Why this redrafting
every season? This shedding of skin?

You are imaginary. Dead, actually. Is that the same thing? Your sister is real. Her name means *alive*. Ironic, isn't it? I've named you after wildflowers even so, your wildness never tamed by the cauldron of birth, the mortal predictability of skin. Sometimes, I think it a blessing. What pain it is to live! The searing pink of the invasive rhododendron in the sun, burning islands embellishing turquoise seas, streets of water, the low hum of a hoverfly's curious flight in a manicured garden. Despite the hurt, I wanted this world for you. To give it to you like a blackberry from a bush, ripe and juicy. It went wrong. *Something* went wrong. It's not my fault, they say. Well-meaning people, darlings, can set a bomb off in your heart no matter how careful they are. *When will you have another one?* I've tried everything. In an alternate life I'd have a brood. Bunkbeds. Cups with all your names on them cluttering the shelves like chickens in a coop. I would be adequate to the task, I suppose, and maybe not even that. But I would hold your little bodies and kiss you goodnight, whisper in the soft shells of your ears, *it was better you were never born at all.*

TRYING TO EXPLAIN MY ATTENTION SPAN FOR THE FIRST TIME

Like cherry blossom petals on the grass, on the pavement, in your hair on a blustery spring day. Like cherry blossom petals pressed against the window, tiny cat noses. Like skin peelings from your healing sunburn falling snow on the carpet. Like discarded clothes on a bedroom floor – explosions of socks and knickers. Like nail clippings twanging across the room at the shock of the scissors' sharp blades. Like spilled cereal smattering on a porcelain tiled floor, the sound of rain. Like light diffusing through a prism, breaking into red, orange, yellow, green, blue, indigo, violet.

(ultraviolet/infrared)

Like crumbs of bread on the lake before the hungry swans peck them up. Like the cygnets too – tiny wisps of grey cloud bobbing across the water. Eight of them, over there. Can you see?

UNASKED FOR ADVICE IS CRITICISM

Don't tell me how to suck eggs.

A SÉANCE TO CONTACT MY DEAD BABIES

Ectoplasm babies, would they do?
I decide yes, and watch
the medium being strapped into the cabinet,
a vertical coffin of sorts.
In the quasi dark her mouth is gaping
as she is shut in.
The circle assembles
to embarrassing music.
Earnestness is the worst –
we all sing along desperately
until the guide possesses her.
Golden Star is an old woman.
'Dear friends, dear, dear friends.'
I sense she is weary.
Who wouldn't be, trying to unite
this world and that
when no one is listening.
Then Cassie, the child, squeaks,
'I'm here! I'm here!' to make us laugh.
If I had a knife
I would stab myself.

The circle urges us to raise
the vibrations.
We must sing, clap,
concentrate.
'Sing, sing you silly billies.'
Oh shut up, Cassie.
Then Moll arrives,
a different voice,
deep and soothing.
Middle-aged.
She will guide them in.
I am restless as a toddler.
I keep applauding,
my palms burn.
The medium says,
'Goo goo gaa gaa.'
Then, 'Mama.'
Out of her nose and mouth
it emerges – ectoplasm –
alive, elastic, rushing
under the cracks in the cabinet
towards me.

All four, suddenly,
solid now, draped
in this substance
enabling them to be here –
real, in front of me.
'Your babies,' she heaves.
My babies back to me,
my four girls.
What a relief!
Come, my muslin children,
my egg yolk infants.
Come my babies made
of soap and gelatine,
of plastic paste, of tissue,
my bouncing bundles
of fine, fine threads.

Like the eyes of a snail
they retract when I try
to gather them to me,
then rematerialize. I try
to pinch a smooth cheek,
the medium squeals.
My babies smell
like animal liver
and evolve,
sometimes incandescent,
sometimes opaque.
I start to cry.
I want to hold them,
but they are out of reach
extensions of the medium's body
not mine. Another failure, alone again,
I stay empty in this breach.

A BRIEF HISTORY OF EASTER EGGS

A formerly forbidden food during Lent,
eggs were painted and decorated to mark the end
of penance, of fasting.
Sometimes dyed red to mimic the blood that Christ
shed during his crucifixion, then given as gifts –
bloody, bloody eggs.
I've always hated them, unless disguised
in cake, or cake. The eggshell is the tomb of course,
the chick inside, Our Lord, cheeping through the crack
imprinting on whomever He happens to see first.

During Holy Week the chickens just kept laying
so the decoration on the shell gave away the age
of these symbols of freshness and fertility.
In this case, old, in this case,
last Holy Week's news.
Give me a break, and a chocolate one any day.
I like to hold the whole, hollow egg in my hand,
listen to the silence inside, beyond the foil and dark shell
and bang it over and over on the table,
until it shatters.

ULTRASOUND ON VALENTINE'S DAY

It's not exactly how I imagined it, in fairness,
though here I am spreadeagled on a bed all the same,
legs open wide as a mouth
taking a deep breath in and out
and in ---
ouch.
I stare at the ceiling,
tell the radiographer
I'm fine, I'm fine.
She is very attentive.
Her name is Girlie
which is perfect.
Occasionally, I tear my gaze
away from the square tiles
above me and try to interpret
the feeling in her dark brown eyes.
I ask her if she can tell me anything.
She laughs like I am insane.
I am, to be honest.
I mean it, I am.
I've been walking around
in a dream, lips hanging open
waiting for words to find me,
for meaning to find me.
Control – ha!
Love – ha!
What about a swollen abdomen,
what about tingling thighs?
What about a heart that's cracked open,
what about dry, sore eyes?
What about the pelvis,

what about that?
Light-headedness, that too.
Idiot, you silly girl.
You haven't got a clue.
You walked into it like a bit,
a roast, a clown. Here again the punchline,
yes, there's blood in your urine,
red-red as a fresh, lovely rose.

Sooner   or later
    the womb becomes
a prison –   cramped & dark.
    The eggshell too
a trap –   it must crack.
    Send us out
from home   into empty air.
    Who knows
(*Pythagoras*!)   what we'll find
    out there?

Not coffins, but boxes
neat and small enough
to be lined up
in chronological order
on the desk I escape to
upstairs in Kerry Library.

The paper inside
each one burnt
with age emits a bitter
smell that turns
sweet when exposed
to the air. Pages

as fragile as skin,
as thin. Words
and letters typed,
scrawled, printed,
shaped by a very
careful child's hand,

pile up. So many
leaflets, postcards,
and copybooks,
labelled *exercise books*,
where students practice
remembering

for those who do not
wish to, blood turned
blue and black instead
along horizontal lines.
Moving forward. Divided
into sections, these accounts

numbered, with the mistakes
crossed out but still
visible as the eye moves
over each page, names
and dates arranged,
a repository of pain.

SECTION 1

a. Collected by _____, as told by _____ and _____, and other members of the _____ family.

b. Song given to _____ by her mother _____.

c. _____ gave the following song to her daughter, _____.

d. The following account of _____ incidents was given to _____ of _____ by _____.

e. As recorded by _____ in conversation with _____.
f. _____ gave the following information to _____.
g. _____ got the following information from _____.
h. Told by _____ to _____.
i. Told to _____ by _____.
j. Collected by _____ as told by _____, _____ and other members of the _____ family.

SECTION 2

We were often out   at night   blocking roads   knocking bridges

SECTION 3

Sad is the story in Kerry today   ~~They beat them up and cut off their~~   *hair To this day he is stone deaf in both ears   Uisce faoi thalamh*   ~~They used the pump to wash off the~~   *blood No means whatsoever   A complete wreck, unfit for any work   Hopelessly insane   Neurasthenic*   ~~No middle path~~   *We are near starving*

SECTION 4

What in God's Holy name am I to do? / What in God's name am I supposed to do?

SECTION 5

One pile for receipts   one for pension books   another for begging letters

Do I fit the eligibility criteria?   One relative gets a pension, the other doesn't

I am an encumbrance to myself and everyone   Even in death hounded and tortured by bureaucracy

It is money that kills   the paper   the lack of   paper   the papers

SECTION 6

I can't think of any more because I am getting old

SECTION 7

I have been given advice: The B_____ M _____ is unavoidable but I must avoid it.

I avoid it.

SECTION 8

I become increasingly alert. There are monuments everywhere. I drive past them too quickly.

SECTION 9

I cannot get the phrase *war of friends* out of my head.

SECTION 10

Group work for Secondary School History students to promote co-operative learning when studying the Irish Civil War:

1. Imagine you were there, what would you do?
2. Write a letter to one of the participants/witnesses/soldiers/civilians out-lining your thoughts on the events. What advice would you give them?
3. What side of the conflict would you be on? Give reasons for your answer.
4. Quantify and discuss individual/family/generational/ancestral trauma in your own life.
5. Compare and contrast this trauma to others you know.
6. Make a timeline.

7. Construct a poster.
8. Draw a diagram.
9. Write a poem.
10. Haven't we all suffered enough?

When I pack up the boxes
one elderly page slashes my finger.
I am terrified it will bleed over everything.
I work quickly to reseal that which cannot be contained. I have been so careful to memorise the placement of each piece of paper. I have certainly gotten it wrong but healing allows for a wound.

I SUPPOSE IT'S POINTLESS TO THINK OF YOU AT ALL
'Parliament Hill Fields', Sylvia Plath

Little one, I must spool it all back, the birth story,
the first feed, your sister holding you
in her sweet arms, the picture of you both
wearing matching dresses on my WhatsApp
profile picture, her loving you, the new branch reaching out
on the family tree for her to catch, to swing from.
Sweet Jesus, the loneliness,
a lump of coal in my stomach. All those Christmases
deleted too. How to figure out who I am
without you –
I project your minuscule squally body.
A secret showing, an intimate screening
that I can replay, and replay, and replay
until the lights flicker out.

/SHELL

WATCHING YOUR EGG CRACK

If the egg was a lightbulb
and the lightbulb glimmered above your head,
shining, bright, yolk-coloured,
a beacon, lighthouse in the dark
and then the light, the yolk, the glass,
cracked
and flooded, trickled, tinkled, crumbled
down so you were covered in it,
new or something,
present or something,
oh my god,
real or something
and the lights all over the house winked
and my tiny, tired heart jolted too –
such voltage
such a shock
     a shock
         a shock.
Darling, why are you so fucking shiny?
Why do you blind me?
Pieces, pieces, everywhere,
on the floor,
in my hair.
Who has been hiding in there?
Folded up like a box in a box.
Nowhere for me to fit,
just goop everywhere, albumen,
the chalazae cords, the useless
fucking embryo.

BJÖRK ON BJÖRK'S SWAN DRESS

They wrote about it
           like
           I was
           trying
           to wear
           a black
           Armani
           and got it
           wrong, like
           I was trying to fit in.
           Of course, I wasn't trying to fit in.

THE HUSBAND SUIT

Wound up like a doll in a jewelry box
    I spin and spin
        – look at myself
           in the tiny rectangular mirror –
             fleetingly –
                dream of you with your soft, long-lashed
                  blue eyes, the veins high
                    and noble in your arms, and that look
                  of furrowed determination to
                stop the rotation, to give me peace.
              Ha! A mirage, a holograph, filled-
           in like paint-by-numbers – a version
        of a husband quiet and calm, silent
      and hard-working, smart and stiff.
He was lovely, we both thought so.
How beautifully constructed,
I didn't even see the stiches, how the suit
      frayed near the pockets. I was spinning, you see.
        So, so, so fast. And his face, well
           it looked just right speeding by, and the
              animal warmth of his hands seeking to grab me.
                And those lips, how we softened into each other
                  on each turning only to be ripped apart.
                Again. *Turn it off, turn it off*, I would
              yell and he would nod but keep winding,
           in his pleasant grey pinstripe cashmere
        with a blue tie the exact colour of the sky
      on our wedding day and of his sequined eyes.
    And what now that a thread from the suit got caught,
and that it ripped right through the fabric from ankle to neck
    and that it stopped my spinning
    and made us see in the stillness
    that you were no husband at all?

ON WONDERING WHETHER TO EXPUNGE THE WORD HUSBAND FROM MY PREVIOUS POEMS

I go back and count
the number of times
I have used the words
husband, he, my husband
in my poems.

It isn't very often,
but I am struck by what
that *H* represents.
Perpendicular lines
the walls. That horizontal

boxing us in. I thought I was happy, I thought he was happy too.
boxing us in. I thought I was happy, I thought he was happy too.

that structure didn't hold,
it collapsed, just like the straw
house, like the stick house
when the wolf blew and blew.
There are no bricks anymore.
I am not the wife, that W
a rollercoaster

of a letter –
I've fallen down its side.
I promise I won't use that word
again for you. I am glad
your new name makes you happy,
the way *husband*
never could.

VAULT OF OBSOLETE PRONOUNS AND DEFUNCT DESCRIPTORS

~~Husband~~
~~husband~~
~~husband~~
~~husband~~
~~husband~~
~~husband~~

~~He he he he~~
~~he he he he~~
~~he he he he~~
~~he he he he~~
~~he he he he~~

~~his his his his~~
~~his his his his~~
~~his his his his~~
~~his his his his~~
~~his his his his~~

Select all images with

crosswalks

Please select all matching images.

VERIFY

SILVER SWAN AUTOMATON

Do not weep for me for I have decanted
all that I am into a clockwork music box.
I am a silver swan now and I sit in a stream
of glass rods and silver leaves, with silver fish
swimming around me. The water looks
like it's flowing when you wind me up.
I turn my head, I preen, I even notice the fish.
Watch how I bend down to catch and eat it.
And then stop and wait until 2pm each day.
At least I did, until the virus locked you out
and I seized up. Do not weep for me, I have
been withdrawn for further conservation.
It's what I've always wanted.

SPILT MILK

Look, it is all over the floor!
See how it runs into the grouting?
Reckless!

It's a mess.
           We have to clean it.
           We have to clean it.
           You have to clean it,

I don't even like milk.
Get to it.
Right now, please!

This minute.
           Or you know what will happen
           and I can't stand that smell,
           the turn, it makes me sick.

The stink,

the sourness of it.
Disgusting!
Stop your crying.

Get the rag!

           Mop it up.
           Mop it up.
           Mop it up.

ALLOW ME TO EXPLAIN THROUGH THE MEDIUM
OF METAPHOR JUST HOW BADLY IT HURTS

The way a seasoned
haberdasher rips fabric –
first making one
tiny incision with
an extremely sharp scissors
then using the power
of their entire arm to tear
along a straight line
so hard and fast you can hear
the shred, see tiny threads
reaching out
from each swathe
of cloth –
one still on the roll
the other loose
going god knows where
to make god knows what
by the yard –
the way they fold it up
into a tiny square
the thread pressed
in against itself
in a small plastic bag
suffocating in layers
and layers
not knowing what will
become of it –
that

'HUMILATED (SWAN)' 2013 BY TRACY EMIN

I doubt it could be any whiter. The box is rectangular as a pat of butter
but chalky, there is no spreading that. It is so brilliant it is embarrassing,
it knows it too, HUMILATED scrawled like a curse across it.
I'd be HUMILATED too. I am HUMILATED but what of it?
It's so old-fashioned it makes me want to cry. I can barely
bring myself to look at the tiny bird floating on top, tucked into
the far-right corner – an oversight, but over everything.
Squinting, I imagine I can almost see the fingerprints that made her,
left her beak just so. I whisper to her about my past so earnestly,
my spittle sprays her plaster plumage. At least she's wet. I tell her
about my mistake. Do I have another choice? Here, there is nothing
left but you. Here, there is nothing left of you.

Here, there is nothing left for you. Here, there is nothing left
for me I am so licked crimson with shame.

HEDGEHOG PRACTISES BEING A WOMAN

I try to jump the stream
in leg warmers that have grabbed
the attention of every bramble
on the climb up that hill.

Water you cleared in one
magnificent deer-leap
I trip over, tangled, too slow,
to fall flat at your feet.

I shut my eyes
as if you will not see
my embarrassment
of ripped leggings,

exposed knicker elastic,
stripes of wet mascara
splitting my face.
My boots, so lately pristine,

two mucky drunks huddling
to my chest in a nest of reeds
and thorns, already dreaming
of the night before.

I curl, hunch my back
into natural roundness
feel them emerge,
shove through skin, paper–

thin, I can't help it—
my spikes, my spikes pop
the silence, shred fabric: you stand
over me, mouthing like a fish,

we were just going for a walk!
Pulling me to my feet, you guide me
back the way we came, all pins
and needles. Once over the gate,

safe on asphalt, my face hot
and drizzly, you laugh
and laugh when I confess
a deep abiding love for paths.

SUPER KING

There is a corpse on our bed.
It is Jesus, down from the cross,
the blood spattered across
his rippling torso, the crown of thorns
ripping the pillow slip and the flesh
on his forehead. I don't know why
He is here, with *that* heart
exposed, His eyes
closed. He *is* dead,
I think. But you know how men
can be, they say
one thing, and the next thing you know
they're on the road
showing off their open wounds
while back at home
the women weep.

ARK OF THE CONVENIENT

Tell me it isn't strange,
this hammering at the door?
It's an excuse to stay in
your arms and knot;
to not go outside into the
stammering wind.
Frustrated gusts unable
to pronounce spring
blow rings around our house
(*our* house) want to come in
or drive us out like
yellow paddle boats
sucked up out of the lake,
forsaken, hilarious as ducks in a row.
The vents rattle vicious rumours
in the living-room, the spare too,
and our picket wooden gate
has fallen – pick it up.

Why is February roaring
and weeping these huge drops?
Dumped by March (the bastard)
or disappointed by January (who isn't?)
You know her best,
reason with her, or put on the kettle;
our electricity works.
I'm glad we live
on a rented hill.
Then come back to bed,
it's global-warm right here.
Let the continental drift,
let it bang and stamp.
We'll line up,
in pairs,
one of you,
one of me,
eventually.

THE EGO IS CRUSHED LIKE A SNAIL SHELL UNDER A STILETTO AND IS BEGRUDGINGLY DIVESTED OF ITS OWN SMUGNESS

When you slipped out of your skin,
you slip of a thing,
the skin I thought I knew you in, it was dazzling
and terrifying. How I too had to slough
wifehood off my dry arms, scrub it from my violently
blue-white legs, exfoliate its unmistakable musk.
You were no more my husband than any other woman.
What a thing to miss! And yet, and yet I tried to imagine
clinging to you like a 1980s polyester nightie sparking in the dark
for God's sake, images of bodies reaching over the mantlepiece
and going up in flames, people chimneys, burned on my child-brain.
Maybe I could do it, and clutch all that we made tightly
until my fists shook. Stupid, smug ego snail. Who am I now
without you but what I have always been, a white feather
in the wind. I told you that when we met, and you cupped me
in your hands – loosely and the wind could blow
at any gale, get knotted, and sure I'd toss a bit, and shiver,
but I could mull that over in the dark, in the dark, in the dark –
did you know? Did you know? They all ask, questions like prodding
fingers. Have they stripped their spouses' skin clean?
Have they watched something fall away –
a lie, no.
A pretence, no.
A realisation, yes.
An epiphany, definitely.
What a ridiculous question though
when you didn't know and dressed as best you could
in what you thought you should. We were just playing
I suppose, until it was clear that it was serious as murder.

The end of us, I mean.
The dream of us.
Not your slinky escape from your chrysalis, not
your beautiful fluttering into the light.

OBLIGATORY INSTAGRAM FOUND POEM

Stop
Thinking
About
Everything
So Much.
You're
Breaking
Your
Own Heart.

LESSONS IN NEUROPLASTICITY WHEN CHANGING YOUR NAME TO YOUR NAME

The telephone is torture.
                    When I call you
I hear you still, as you were, on your voicemail
                    and my brain persists in thinking
nothing has changed.
                    I update to your new name
in my contacts. It is a shock
                    every time you call.
Who is she?

TO THE SWAN THAT HAS FALLEN IN LOVE WITH A PEDALBOAT IN GERMANY

It is not your typical love story, you must admit.
I've seen the news report, you're famous,
and watched how you, bizarrely named Black Peter –
    (I am sorry, how rude.
    It's a lovely, appropriate name
    for a black female swan) –
have got it bad; it must have been some spring,
no wonder you refuse to fly south.
I'll be honest, he's easy on the eye,
if you ignore the two humans pedalling furiously,
and he's almost six feet high.
The owner of your love has agreed to relocate
you both to a zoo for the winter months.
An unusual match, the news reporter said,
but they seem to be enjoying their new home.
Black Peter, never did I think I would understand.
I wintered with a man-shape,
beautiful girl hidden inside, steering away,
screaming, and I didn't hear a thing.

ART GALLERY EASTER EGGS

Join me, won't you, as I tour the galleries of the world.
I will be crawling along those silken, parquet floors
like an animal on all fours, a runting thing, sliding
under the artworks I do not deserve to observe.
But please bear with me, bear with me, because
I've noticed things, things I have noticed might be
of interest to you as they eluded me for so long,
Easter eggs you see, Easter eggs to tease and please,
for the clever ones, the ones that pride themselves
on looking. I used to be one, God knows, and what
a joke it is to be staggered by your own life – a little
Easter egg of my own but that's too soon. Allow me
to point you instead in the direction of *Death and
Ascension of St. Francis* by Giotto with my hoof,
(I am not worthy even of a claw.) Let me show you
the image lurking in the cloud of vapour, a portrait
with a hooked nose, sunken eyes, with two
dark horns – it isn't me, but the devil with a smarmy
grin. That's not all, here's Michelangelo's *The Creation
of Adam* in the Sistine Chapel – the floor is lava – but above
us the swooping cloak folds itself into the shape of an
anatomically correct human skull. Don't ask Michelangelo
how he knows what that looks like, marvel instead
at the brain stem, the spinal cord in palimpsest along
the throat of God in *The Separation of Light and Darkness*.
I don't understand mathematics but appreciate them
enough to wonder at Dürer's *Melancholia* that houses
a magic square right up in the right there, that no matter
what achieves perfect numerical balance, thirty-four,
a symbol of the divine and in counterbalance to the saturnine
temperament. I could go on – *The Ambassadors* by Holbein

the Younger conceals then reveals an imposing skull.
Never forget Caravaggio hid his own tormented face
on Goliath's severed head. Look at Metsu's abandoned
shoe! My favourite is van Gogh's *Café Terrace
at Night* – yes, that is Jesus, yes, serving twelve
charming customers under the awning, behind
Him the window frames are cross-like so he is crucified
again and again by candlelight. I am exhausted. This is quite a long
poem. I am gasping and coughing up phlegm on the steps of
the Kröller-Müller Museum. Look away, it's disgusting.
I am disgusted with myself, my whole body made
of Easter eggs, my life a Christian festival of denial
and excess. Yes, I see it now, from the beginning the eggs,
they were everywhere. I was distracted, you see, by the figures,
how handsome, the paint strokes, so skilful, and by
the many, many beautiful colours.

LISTENING BACK TO PHONE RECORDINGS I MADE IN THE CAR WHILE TRYING TO DRIVE AWAY FROM MY LIFE

I don't want to do it; I don't want to do it.

I've been so good.

I came to the sea to see the mountains and the windmill, but the mist has taken them away.

I am sitting in the drizzle; I can't see anything.

No horizon. No mountains. No windmill.

I don't want to do it.

How am I supposed to do it?

POEM IN WHICH I WISH I WORE EMILY DICKINSON'S DRESS INSTEAD

It was silk.
Fluid as a promise, cascading
down my body, a dream
in cream. Emily, there were mother-
of-pearl tablets ringing the neck-
line that shimmered and glowed
opaquely – classy you see.
I thought I was a bride – there was
a veil – a veil with a train that flowed
and followed me, loyal and persistent
down the aisle,
its net gathering, gathering.
Did I tell you I thought I was a bride?
      Even my heart was pearl-coloured,
      an oyster's gift pried open and bare,
      bloodless
      but what a mess. It turns out, Emily
      it was a ghost's gown, a dead
      poet's garb because all I can do
      is write about it as it whispers vows
      from the dark wardrobe in the next room.
      I can't bear to look at it,
      my own little haunting,
      my own dead costume.

VICTORIA RE-ENACTS THE STATIONS OF THE CROSS. (DON'T WE ALL?)

(1) Victoria is condemned to the truth, there is no way around it.

(2) She is made to bear this cross and develops TMJ.

(3) Victoria falls the first time, down the stairs, spilling coffee all over herself.

(4) She tells her mother about her marriage, her broken marriage.

(5) Victoria's family and friends are made to bear the cross by listening to her process this information. They are sainted.

(6) Her sister wipes her face and tells her to brush her teeth and be in bed by 10pm. She does not drink enough water.

(7) Victoria falls the second time, the stairs again I swear, and must go to A&E. She is fine, the doctor was *fine*.

(8) She goes for dinner with the girls and cries twice, they do not roll their eyes.

(9) Victoria falls the third time; this is getting ridiculous.

(10) She is scared to get rid of the male clothes and old baby clothes stuffed secretly into drawers. To say goodbye to an imagined life. Instead, she buys herself new clothes in sizes she does not approve of. They fall out of the wardrobe like dead bodies.

(11) Victoria is nailed to the cross, or rather she nails herself.

(12) She dies, many times over. This is the truth, you see.

(13) Victoria takes herself down from the cross[1]

(14) She lies on her bed, alone, and sighs. In three days, she will take up Pilates.

---

[1]   See 'Modern Crucifixion' for more details.

MODERN CRUCIFIXION

Yes
Yes
Yes
Yes yes yes yes yes
Yes
Yes
Yes

No. Not any more
I am standing on my own   two broken feet now,
                                     stomping.

CENSUS NIGHT POEM

I cry every time. I am so small.
We are all so small and tonight we know it.
Don't you want to run barefoot in your dressing-gown
into your neighbours' house and say,

Hello, I love you!
Here we are on this rock together!
Hold my hand, hold me.

I want to write down the names of all my dead relatives.
How are they not here anymore? How are yours absent too?
What do we do with them, their names? Is there a box for grief?

ORIENTATION: A TRAGEDY

I am so straight I give myself paper cuts.

PELVIS

There's a sheep's pelvis in our garden now, bleached
white as truth, white as purity, white as teeth.
It's bowl-shaped enough to hold up the garden,
our house, the whole sky. I walk by it every day,
going out the back door, sneaking around
my own house, sneaking around my own life.
Not wanting myself to see myself, not wanting to be seen.
To confront another person is the same as confronting
a sheep's pelvis on the step of your own back door.
The shock of another's face. The shock
of another's expectation of you. The shock
at your own face trying to present itself as a face
to converse with. This sheep's pelvis is whitening,
brightening, blanching each passing day,
through the seasons. I cannot move it; it won't be moved.
It will just stay there like the sky, like my face,
                              holding up.

MAD HONEY

I have eaten the mad honey,
there is no saving me.

I lie on the grass,
my clothes stained green,

I am on my death bed, my face
so long. I am toothless, screaming,

without water. No one knows my name,
what I like to wear,

my favourite foods – though food
is irrelevant here. The sheets are depressed,

drooping like earlobes.
I am melting, you see.

I don't want it to be like this.
I am so unevolved. I stretch

my hand out from under the linen.
It is skeletal and terrifying. Elongated.

No one wants to touch me, I am
the embodiment of death. Death is catching.

My brains will liquify, and as they
blancmange I will shout and wail and moan

a name that no longer exists so no one will know
who I mean, and you will not come.

CYGNUS, THE SWAN IN THE STARS

Is there anything to be said
      for gathering your own bones,
being responsible like that, and taking the poor, tired
      and battered corpse of who you once were   from its treacherous
position and giving it a proper burial so it can ascend?
      The sting is there'll have to be a transition from one
form to another, so I take the shape of a swan
      with large powerful wings and a   long slender neck.
My feet webbed to swim to those unimaginable
      depths where my earthly remains lie shattered. I'll retrieve
them and put them in the ground – *She was only human!*
      engraved on my headstone. I am hoping to find   my place
      in the sky, a swan in the stars,
wings spread wide, majestic   immortal.

TEMPERA

1000 Eggs: For Women, 2018 by Sarah Lucas at the
New Museum, New York

There is not the time to tour now,
I am in a rush!
There are so many, too many
eggs painted and sculpted, etched, and inlaid.
I must take

what she has given me
in the gallery. An egg,
a real one from a live bird.
I hold it for a moment, weigh it in my hand,
its fragility, and I do as she tells me.

I throw it
at the wall with all my might.
It is blank white, aren't all blank walls
white? But I can imagine Dali's eggs up there
and all the others too.

Take that. Paganly,
we enacted this ritual before the Christians
turned us all sour – imagine having permission
to play, or not needing or seeking it at all?
Before oil paint and the tyranny of waiting

artists painted frantically
with egg yolk, bound to the terror of time. Now,
in solidarity we bind together to throw the eggs,
a thousand of us, egging the wall, the world,
but we do not make a mess.

We have made
the most beautiful egg painting taking it into
our own hands, this cell, and making the
most intense shade of rich yellow
streaked like the dawn, but inevitably running
vertically,

smelly.
Still
intentional.

CHILD OF LIR
after Alice Oswald

Mother-of-pearl eyes and a mother-of-pearl heart,
it's alright: the movement inside you is the song
of ruffling feathers. Mother-of-pearl mirror,
mother-of-pearl shroud, it is time sweet one
to let your self be. I have a feather in my throat,
so please forgive the words I have said, have yet to say.
I love you, though the plumage that I recognise will moult
away in clumps. Mother-of-pearl soul, a reflection,
please forgive the tears I have shed, have yet to shed.
I want to celebrate with you the hurrying away from
a body that didn't fit. I want to celebrate with you
the escape from clothes that made you dull yourself.
Lift away, climb out and take to the sky in your beautiful
form, familiar and new, your arms are strong and can
always fly. Don't look back if you can at me standing
by the wreckage. I will be weeping like a wife.
A puff of smoke, a magic trick. Did I imagine
my whole life? Strange, my yearnings,
strange that every night I dream of swans now,
their wingbeats, their webbed black feet.
What heaviness I carry as I watch you take off.
Quick, say something to me, frozen as I am
at the lake's lip. I am waiting for nothing
but I feel like I am dying. I want it to snow
so it covers the blood stains. I mutter under
my breath when I see a bride, *Fool, fool,*
as if I am calling my own name. I am sorry,
for all of this, what I am saying now. It is
hard to hurt and then explain the hurt away
so as not to hurt anyone. But have you seen my
life? Where did I put it? Would you like

to try it on? It is so cold and St. John's spire
pokes at the sky for answers. Someone is ringing
the bell, is it you announcing yourself? Your
new name ringing and ringing across the whole
town. Mother-of-pearl memory, mother-of-pearl
angel in the lake, let me close this feeling
as easily as I will close my eyes.

SWAN SONG

It's night-time.
We hold hands,
peer into the hole
we dug together.
Into it we place
our marriage,
the full shape of it,
moon-shiny. An egg,
the seed we have tended
for so long, now
we must bury it.
We are both crying,
of course, but it
must be done.
We pat the earth
with the flat
of our hands,
imagining each other's
backs. A bald, featherless
patch on the grass.
You sing, even so,
our little song.
The mute swans stay mute.

ACKNOWLEDGEMENTS

With thanks to the following publications where a number of these poems, or earlier versions of them, have been published: *New England Review*, *The Poetry Review*, *Poetry Ireland Review*, *Poetry London*, *The Telegraph*, *The Storms Journal*, *The Forward Prize Anthology 2023*, *Versopolis Spanish Anthology 2023*, *Anthropocene Poetry Journal*, *Poetry Birmingham Literary Journal*, *PN Review*, and the *Éire-Ireland*.

The completion of this manuscript was generously supported by a Literature Bursary from the Arts Council of Ireland, a Literature Ireland Artist Residency at the Centre Culturel Irlandais Paris, and a Kerry Arts Council Bursary to attend a Writers' Retreat in Ireland at Greywood Arts, Killeagh, Co. Cork. I am also ever grateful to the Tyrone Guthrie Centre for providing me with time and space to further work on this book, as well as the support of the Yeats Society Sligo, particularly the director, Susan O'Keeffe, while I was Poet in Residence. A huge thank you also to Paul Perry and my friends, students, and colleagues at UCD where I was Arts Council of Ireland Writer in Residence 2023.

I am grateful too for the support of everyone at Literature Ireland, The Poetry Society, the T.S. Eliot Foundation, the Seamus Heaney Centre, Dalkey International Book Festival, Poetry Ireland, Poetry as Commemoration Project UCD, The Munster Literature Centre, The John Hewitt Summer School, West Cork Literature Festival, Manchester Literary Festival, Irish Arts Centre New York, *The Stinging Fly*, Sylvia Plath Festival, The British Library, Tralee County Library, Seamus Heaney HomePlace, Out-Spoken London, Strokestown Poetry Festival, Listowel Writers' Week, Dingle Literary

Festival, Cúirt International Festival of Literature, Belfast Book Festival, the Maria Edgeworth Literary Festival, Bray Literary Festival, The Patrick Kavanagh Festival, Rose Hotel Tralee, The Arvon Foundation and The Poetry School.

My deepest and most sincere gratitude to all at Carcanet Press for making this book a reality, especially Jazmine Linklater, Andrew Latimer, Michael Schmidt, and most of all, to my editor John McAuliffe, who has made everything possible, again. I am so endlessly fortunate to have the benefit of his brilliance, expertise, understanding, insight, and sensitivity at every stage of my creative journey. I also hugely appreciate the close and sensitive reading of this manuscript by Dr. H Gareth Gavin and his insightful, thorough and thoughtful feedback.

To my wonderful family and friends in Kerry and Cork, for their patience, love, advice, encouragement and understanding during this book's composition, especially my sister Louise, my mother Úna, Deborah, and Noel O'Regan (Brain Trust!). And dear, darling, wonderful Vivienne – all of this is for you.

Trans Rights Are Human Rights.